BEST SELF

Self help book for Women to Work on Self Worth, Love and Care, and Discover Inner Happiness

3 Edition

Jennifer Clarke

ISBN - 9798454598914

Content

Introduction

Welcome, my dear readers!

You are holding this book in your hands, which means you are mentally ready to work on improving some aspects of your life. Congratulations! This is the first step!

This book consists of 5 chapters, each representing an important aspect of self help: Self Love, Positive Thinking, Balance in life, Communication, and Recreation. Read it through and practice advice, exercises provided along the way. Apply new knowledge to your current life.

Keep this book by your side, and whenever you have doubts, feel anxiety or need support, inspiration, open and turn to these pages.

The answers you seek are within.

At the end of the book you will find *a Place to save your insights and ideas*. You can write down some thoughts and conclusions, quotes from the book, or just pages you want to come back to. I recommend using that space to help you quickly refresh important points in your memory after.

I wish you good luck on your journey to a higher self esteem, better self care, change of mindset. Applying advice provided in this book, you find harmony among 8 aspects of your life, learn how to improve the quality of communication, and contribute to a higher level of energy by recreating in the right way!

To the new beginnings!

CHAPTER 1. The truth about self love

We start our journey with deepening into such terms as self love and here I will do my best to make sure you realise the value of your life, your personality and existence, and change your perception of reality at some point. We will define your inner self, work on pain points, any factors blocking you from living the best life, deepen into feelings and emotions and reach the point where you are ready and willing to truly care about yourself, with love and tenderness.

I would say self love is about being brave to realise your wildest dreams, conquer your strongest fears, and go for anything you find worthy to spend time on, go for the Life, and be the best version of yourself during the way.

True self love is expressed when you do everything possible to become the best version of yourself. When you pay attention to your feelings, pains and desires, and not agree to the less. When you care about yourself that much to follow your dreams, create comfort and treat yourself as you want others to treat you.

Self love is in surroundings you choose, food you buy, clothes, shoes, ways of transportation, books you read, people around, health caring, hobbies and habits. Self love is wishing all the best to yourself, and acting the way to improve living conditions and level of life, because you believe you deserve it. People with self love have a healthy high self esteem, that has nothing to do with arrogance.

Arrogance means the person is so concentrated on herself she does not notice the good qualities of others, and when she does, she tries to find proof these others are worse than herself in some other ways. Self love means you totally accept and agree there are many great personalities, many outstanding women out there, but it does not affect your self-treatment, it does not make you feel worse about yourself. It might just be a stimula for development, an idea for self growth, but not the reason to treat yourself any worse.

True self care is expressed in these small details, like not eating a slice of pizza when you are not hungry and there are alternatives. Not eating a slice of pizza not because you can put on weight and others will like you less, but because you care about yourself that much not to feed your body unhealthy food. Because you wish yourself all the best, and that is why you care about body and spirit.

Deep self love and self esteem are closely related since realising the true value of your life and personality inevitably impacts the way you "evaluate" and treat yourself.

Numerous studies have shown how important it is to take time out for ourselves every day, and how not doing so can lead to anxiety, depression, low self esteem, and losing ourselves. There should be an element of self care day after day in your life, so that you feel calm, relieved and happy no matter what.

Creating everyday self care rituals is a great start and a meaningful investment in the improvement of life quality. That is a chance to make a peaceful regular point during the day, when your mind would receive a signal to relax and take a pause. Everyday ritual might be a meditation, exercising, art therapy in the evening, a morning walk around neighborhoods etc. Beauty routine might also be a ritual if it makes you feel good and relieved. I would recommend trying to implement one ritual at a time and keep an eye on following it for a couple of weeks every day, to create a habit.

In a hectic world like this, it is crucial for people to have calm, quiet moments to give the brain a break. Having everyday rituals helps keep concentration and reduce stress, since no matter what happens you know you will come back home and do yoga (as an example). It creates a so-called safety zone for you that helps you feel protected and know what is going on in life. I am elaborating this topic in Chapter 3: In search of harmony - meditations, yoga, mindfulness.

Mood, emotions and Self Love

I believe learning how to understand and control emotions is an important step on the way to self love. Emotions affect the way we feel all the time, our mood is determined in the way we feel. That is how treatment to life and perception of how good or bad our life is directly impacts moods, emotions, feelings. We can develop this skill to control, change, manage our mood, emotions.

So why don't we give it a shot and work on that skill?

Let's start from a simple question:

How are you feeling right now?

Knowing how you feel is the first step towards controlling your emotions.

Can you call that state of mind somehow, can you classify it?

Can you understand reasons why you feel this way? I mean actually explain where that exact mood comes from?

Seat still, put the book away for a moment, and try to think, analyze.

How emotions are formed

Interpretation + Identification + Repetition = Strong Emotion

---

This formula is introduced by Thibaut Meurisse. Interpretation means your perception of a situation or an event, thought etc. based on your background.

Identification means your first-second treatment and defined pattern of how to react.

Repetition means regular occurrence of a situation and the same reaction from your side.

Understanding of how the strong emotion is formed helps you find reasons and prerequisites of treatment you have. When you understand Why you treat certain people or situations in a particular way, it gives you control over your feelings.

To simplify the process of following how your mood was changing over time, I recommend trying to use a Mood tracker.

Not only mood defines your treatments and demonstrates appearing emotions, it also plays a significant role in accomplishing tasks, meeting deadlines, and having energy for living, you can help yourself by tracking its changes and following the reasons why it changes.

Human beings are emotional creatures, and our actions are more or less controlled by impulses, one-second wishes, and external factors. Being depressed, sad, weak, or angry would definitely affect your productivity and motivation to work hard. Although, sometimes people do not consciously notice that something is wrong. They might be disappointed because of some problems in relationships, might feel depressed because of spending too much time on social media and comparing themselves to others, or feel sick but not pay attention to that. What happens is a person still requires oneself to be productive, and have the same amount of work done, although she is not able to do that because of those factors making her feel bad. And instead of solving problems, taking rest, treating herself, she tries even harder to make herself do stuff, and a lot of energy is wasted, plus the person feels horrible.

The mood tracker would serve as a small reflection point in the evening, to pay attention to how you felt today, and analyze the mental condition during the day.

I believe using a mood tracker is a way to care about yourself, and have a picture demonstrating the level of happiness/ satisfaction at the end of the month.

Monthly mood trackers usually include 31 sections for each day of the month and a zone where you decide what colors mean particular moods.

My Mood

Today
I
Felt...

Energetic, Motivated   Happy   Content, Neutral

Sad   Anxious   Tired, Annoyed   Angry   Weak, Sick

To fill it in every day you need highlighters, markers or colour pencils, colour pens. You use each colour for each mood, and can choose your favorite colour for «happy» feeling, as well as some dark or unpleasant colour for «sad», «anxious».

Moreover, when analyzing your mood state every day, there is a high chance that your mood the day after would be better! It happens often when people are feeling sad or unmotivated because they are bored, and realising it in the evening would help to have a better mood the next day.

When you start thinking about how you felt, you might find out your mood was changing during the day. It would be nice to spend a couple of minutes analyzing what exactly was the factor to change your mood for the better, or for the worse. This way, you might find out the things you can easily remove from your daily routine, or move them to the other part of the day, to feel better.

You get all these benefits by simply filling in one piece of paper every day. Worth trying, huh?

It is also possible that after a month or two, your mood during the day statistically will be more stable than before. Why? Because by reflecting on your mental state every evening you will learn how to listen to yourself, notice bad impacts, and avoid it.

Why should we care about tracking and noticing our mood patterns? Well, because the way we feel impacts the way we think. And the way we think determines the actions we take, which in turn influences our experiences and ultimately, our feelings, events in life.

Such practice is highly recommended for people suffering from the first stages of depression, teenagers, and people having issues with anxiety, low self-esteem, or going through tough periods of life. It would also help the people who live in stress, are too busy to concentrate on the feelings, and do not know how to stop. You do not need to have such problems to start using a mood tracker though. Getting and keeping a stable and healthy mental state requires constant efforts and acts of caring about yourself.

When you understand your emotions, you can use them as a powerful guide over your life, since they show when something is wrong and can help fix issues you don't like about the current situation. Controlling emotions helps avoid overreacting, but rather use emotions as an indicator of what you don't like, and have time to think on how to change it.

Our brain is built in the way we pay more attention to dangers or negative, irritating factors, than we do to safety, positive feelings and comfort. Hundreds of years ago it was necessary for survival. People had to be always ready for a danger, or they would die. The world has changed, but our attention subconsciously is still divided in the way to identify "what is wrong". As much as pessimistic it sounds, we search for bad things, and often ignore good ones, take them for granted, and notice their importance only when they are missing. There is nothing wrong with you in particular to do that, that is human nature.

However, since we are smart creatures, we can learn to manually switch the focus of our attention, get a habit to notice positive vibes, factors and people around us, and make life better, and self-esteem higher thanks to that.

Are you following me?

It is not a feature people get, although that is a skill we can learn while caring about ourselves.

Let's figure out how.

Again, your brain gives significantly more weight to adverse events than to positive ones. Fear of rejection is one example of a bias toward negativity. (And a thing you definitely should know while learning how to love yourself). See, hundreds of years ago being rejected by a tribe you were born in hardly meant death, because people couldn't survive without a united mechanism of hunting for food, keeping the fire, caring about food and so on. They needed a group, and whoever ended up alone, would have his chances to survive drop significantly. Nowadays, a person does not necessarily have to be in a group to survive. He or she can have a job, home, food that is now easy to get from the store, same as cloth, and other necessary things. Although, our brain is still programmed to perceive rejection as a threat to survival.

You might know most rejections are not going to influence your life and comfort, but you still feel emotional pain, and may create the whole drama around it, concluding you are not worthy of love. One critical statement about your appearance or personality can outweigh dozens of positive ones.

This is why it is important to know about such features of our mind and learn how to notice these instincts, and take control over them. Change your treatment manually, do not follow natural panic.

Fear of rejection produces overthinking and creating drama in situations nothing bad was standing behind. You are fortunate to have these survival reactions, although you have to learn on your own to separate real threats from imaginary ones.

Fears. Practice

Find one example of imaginatory threat resulting from your survival mechanism. Describe it, try to realise how it takes control over your mind.

How would you avoid it next time?

Do you think knowing about its nature would help you feel safer next time you are in a similar situation?

Mood. Practice.

Think about the mood for the day as of the cloth you choose in the closet:

You take a hanger with a dress or a shirt, you go to the mirror, and try it on. You think about the way you want to look today.

Try the same with the mood: you wake up in the morning, and try to realise what kind of person you want to be today, what you want to feel, what impression you want to make on other people. Smile and make a conscious decision.

Do that tomorrow morning. You do not even need to believe it works. All you need to do is to Try. Here: take your phone and make a reminder for tomorrow morning: "Choose a mood". Do that in the bed, while drinking coffee, or putting cloth on. Try to notice if you stick to it during the day, and in the evening estimate how well you performed. Stay patient and do that every morning for 2 weeks, and I swear, you will see the difference.

When you actually see the difference, please take 2 minutes and write a comment to the book on Amazon, letting me know it works for you. Thanks! :)

"*It's too simple to be true.*" I've heard it soo many times. But it IS simple. You should Decide to be happy. You should be absolutely sure you deserve to be happy. You are the only person who can actually change your mood, and make you happy in the end. See? So simple, but hard at the same time.

Here is one more practice I recommend you all to think about and try in your life.

I am pretty sure you have already heard something about "magic morning" and the importance of starting the day right. Hearing about something, thinking, or even planning is not the same as practicing, unfortunately. In this book, I am not gonna make you wake up at 5 am (or any other particular time), not gonna tell you exactly what to do and in what order. I will give you general advice and my own example of a pleasant and full-of-energy morning (not a to-do list, just one of multiple ideas).

Let me present an example first, and insights and outputs after.

My Morning Routine

I wanna share with you, my dear readers, my personal, verified on practice, tutorial on how to make my day Better, how to live the next day deliberately and feel pleasure, getting things done.

The best thing is to start from the night before. It's simple and won't take much time. Let's say you are in bed and ready to fall asleep: close your eyes and try to imagine the next day. Be realistic here, but make an effort to add as many smiles, pleasant moments and happiness as possible. Keep in mind the things that are to be done tomorrow, And free of duties time you have. Wonderful if you can go step by step and imagine every activity focusing on details, people and tastes, smells. Now you can sleep.

In the morning your task is to find 10-15 minutes when nobody disturbs you -- if you have a big family, or work early mornings,it's a good idea to wake up 15 minutes earlier. (Trust me, it's worth it). So, you wake up, wash your face/brush teeth, and then go to some place (a balcony, backyard, cozy windowsill, square near your house), sit comfortably, and tune in for the day. You can come up with your own ritual, morning routine, that makes you feel good and includes things you love.

Here is my example: I wake up 25 minutes before sunrise, slide down from my bed, put on some cloth, and go to the kitchen -- to make coffee.

Making coffee is my small ritual: I listen to some positive music, stretch, and completely wake up until the coffee is made. I focus on the smell, put coffee into my travel cup, and go to the roof to watch the sunrise. I enjoy the view, and start mentally preparing for the upcoming day. I think about how to optimize the time, the sequence of my tasks. Then I take my favorite blanket and seat on the grass in a quiet place under the trees: that's the time for meditation. Mostly I meditate with classical music in the morning (Try Oliver Schuster and Ludovico Einaudi).

This morning is filled with love. First of all, to myself -- because I do things I love, the ones that inspire me. And just like that -- I settle a particular mood for the day. Yes, I made an effort to wake up and start my routine, and yes, sometimes I feel lazy and unmotivated, but as soon as I slide down from my bed - I feel proud. That is the most out of morning you can get -- to feel good about yourself. That way, there is a much higher chance your day will be productive, as well as pleasant.

You can try different approaches and come up with your own perfect routine. It should not start at 7 am -- whenever it works for you. The main rule is to do things you love, organise your thoughts, and fill yourself with energy (this way, watching shows in the morning wouldn't work: you may like it, but id does not make you feel better).

Listen to your favorite music, take a walk, go for a run, ride a bike, do stretching, cook a family breakfast, take a shower and put facemask on, meditate -- whatever, but after that you should feel fulfilled, have much energy, and Smile.
You can find advice on how to come up with your own morning ritual on the next page.

Morning routine advice for Beginners

Let's come up with certain "rules", more like a guideline so that you can write down and apply your own ideal morning.

The main goal is to get ready for the day (whatever the day is - working/busy, or relaxing). You need to spend this time to organize your thoughts, imagine the best version of this particular day, balancing the work and the rest, useful things and pleasant things. After doing this practice on a regular basis for a while, you'll learn how to put realistic expectations and not to require too much from yourself.

Secondly, your task is to create the mood for the whole day. Thinking positive, dreaming for a little bit, listening to favorite music, making favorite drinks (not alcohol preferably, but various mornings happen).

Find a spot of something beautiful - anything you like to look at. My ideal spot to spend morning at - is ocean shore, but until the time I can be there every morning - I have sunrises, a park close to the house, a pond, my special bench under the tree. It is not even necessary that you do the exact same things every morning. You may have a set of them, and should know that's something that fills you with strength and energy.

Timing -- 20 minutes to 1 hour I'd say. It may differ for working days and days-off. Let's say you love doing some face procedures in front of the mirror listening to music and dancing. You may not have enough time to make the whole list every morning, but you can do that on Sunday for the whole hour.

You should ENJOY. Just enjoy. Whatever it is. I strongly recommend to get outside during your magic morning time. Although different days may occur, and when it rains hard outside -- let's say you just stay in bed and read a fiction book, having cacao right by you. Sounds good, huh? Definitely better, than being depressed and angry because of the weather.

Everybody has difficulties and moments in life when she is too busy. Your task is not to spoil that small amount of time you can get, and use it to fill yourself with a resource, instead of rewatching stupid show for the third time.

Make a list of what you like generally to define your morning routine. Then think about what things can be done in 15-50 minutes, and make an order. In the morning you should have a strict guide you should follow. Especially, in the beginning

You may also do similar stuff in the evening before going to bed, you can test. Based on my practice, morning works better for most of the people.

Happy - to BE or NOT to BE

Your happiness is determined with the things you focus the attention on. That impacts your behavior and has a direct influence on the level of happiness. Humans always have scarcity of resources, scarcity of attention in this case, this is why you have to be smart while making a decision on how to divide your attention, and what to spend time on. I mean, you should make a conscious decision here.

If you are not happy enough it probably means your focus is slightly on the wrong things, or the level of attention is exceeded there.

An interesting thing about human psychology is that not everyone has to be rich to be happy, because different people pay different amounts of attention to such factors as income. It basically means change your treatment and expectations to a sphere of life, and it will impact your general level of happiness less. So the impact of money on our life depends on how much we think about it, not how much money we have. The same resources - money, sex, marriage, attractive appearence, success -- can impact your feelings in a different way depending how much you care.

It is nothing about me trying to convince you to forget your dreams and life purposes and simply give up, because it might make you unhappy. What I am saying is make a choice: find the way to get what you want and turn that thing into the source of positive emotions, OR change your treatment.

I am ready to pre-open the key to self love, satisfaction and happiness at this point -- to find (and create, add) pleasure in everyday routine.

That is one of the main points of this book. Help yourself, and allow yourself to enjoy everyday life as much as possible. Care about balance of pleasure and meaningfulness, make your life interesting to you, find joy in unexpected places, be in resource and be the reason for your own happiness.

The way you feel about yourself, the way you perceive the world and fulfill your life has a tremendous impact on self love, this is why Happiness is a big part of this chapter. I decided to go deeper and explain a so-called formula of happiness introduced by P. Dolan.

Happiness is a unity of sensations of pleasure and meaningfulness.

Why are these two things so important to human beings?

Why do we suffer when one of them is missing?

Basically, we have 2 types of emotions -- positive and negative. They can either be preconceived, or unconditioned.

We can make such tables to visualize the feelings we have in 4 types of situations.

EMOTIONS	Positive	Negative
Unconditioned	Content, calm	Sad, depressed
Preconceived	Joyful, thrilled	Worried, angry

What does it mean?

Well, here is what you need to learn -- a girl is happy, when she either considers her actions meaningful, or is doing pleasant things.

Although, it is not enough just to enjoy life without doing anything important, or, on the contrary, to devote life to changing the world, and forget about her own feelings.

The secret of happiness lays in the right balancing of doing meaningful things, and pleasant. (Paul Dolan Concept)

Happiness = Meaningfulness + Pleasure

Let's say the firefighter suffers physically, when rescuing people, but at the same time he realises he is doing a very important thing, and that is why he feels good.

A famous writer needs to apply strict self-discipline to finish a book (because her fans are waiting), instead of going to a beach with family -- she wants to get some pleasure of swimming and spending time with her family, feels worried she stays at home, but the feeling of meaningfulness wins at that moment, and in the end of the day she feels joyful she moved closer to the book release.

If the firefighter or the writer in these stories were just doing meaningful things and did not allow themselves to take a rest, to get some pleasure, they would not be that productive, and in the end would not enjoy the work. They need to balance.

At the same time, let's say a housewife has a glamorous life, her husband earns good money and she can do many pleasant things during the working days, since she does not have a job. Although, at some point she starts feeling depressed, as she starts to realise she wastes her life and does not leave anything meaningful after herself. She does not help people in any way, does not have her own children to raise, does not contribute to science, technology progress and so on.

It is always easier to realise what pleasant things you can do to make you feel good. The challenging task is to find what brings you joy from meaningfulness.

There is not an exact formula or checklist on how to find a sense of life, since it varies a lot for different people. The only advice I can give you is to try as many things as possible -- volunteering, social organisations, working due to your major for companies that have similar values as you do, traveling.

You will be getting that understanding gradually, and in the end will find all pieces of puzzle and have the whole picture.

Happiness. Practice

Here is the task for you. Take a piece of paper, and write as many things that make you feel good, and make you feel happy, as possible. You can write down the ones that come to your mind at once, and come back to it in a couple of hours / the next day. Add more items, including global and constant things like caring friendship, and single actions like massage, or eating pizza.

Now take another piece of paper and divide it into 2 sections -- Pleasure, Meaningfulness. Try to classify the things from the list into these 2categories. This way, you find out short-term and long-term factors of your happiness.

Take a look, analyze and remember this table -- it might become a useful guide and impact the way you prioritize tasks in daily life, as well as the way you make long-term plans.

Doing this exercise, you learn more about yourself, and actually care about the future.

Self love is based on many factors including the ability to identify your feelings, fears, treatments, the desire to make yourself feel better and readiness to work a lot to reach your goals, true caring about health, comfort and positive environment.

Working on all of these aspects gradually, looking for passions, opening new angles to look at your personality, will deepen your self love, make you happy and satisfied.

Enjoy the way!

CHAPTER 2. Positive Vibes - How to Stop Overthinking and Start Living

Psychologists conducted the following experiment. They would put people in separate rooms, give them remote controllers, and tell them that they should come up with a sequence of pressing the buttons to get the light on. They would get a score every time they get the light on. The task is to get the score as high as possible for half an hour.

What happened? People would seat down and press all the buttons in a random order till they got light on. Then they would try to recreate what they did before to get the light on for the second time. But it didn't work that way this time. After that participants would try to complicate their actions adding more steps, for example pressing one of the buttons 4 times and skip another one. The light would go on again. It would stop working at some point eventually.

Next thought was "Maybe it's not about buttons? Maybe it's the way I sit? The strength I am pressing the buttons?"

And people would go on and on in their assumptions and in the end, they would leave the room being totally sure they found the right algorithm.

The truth is .. there was no algorithm. The light would go on and off without any reasons, randomly.

What was the purpose of the experiment?

It perfectly demonstrates how the human brain can easily believe in nonsense, and after persuade itself that is the only possible scenario. Every participant would leave the room persuaded he knew how to score in that game. These algorithms were totally different, but all of the participants would think theirs is the only possible way to get the light on.

When we see (or we think we see) some pattern, some regularity in everyday life, it doesn't take much time from us to conclude that related features we notice - matter, we make a big deal out of nothing and then tell everyone that's a rule, the only possible way to (make friends, earn money, get married, teach a child eat etc.).

It happens because our brain constantly looks for a sense. In anything. And when there is no sense in certain events or behaviors, we overthink and imaginarily add this sense there. We press the button, see the lights go on, and decide it happened because we pressed the button. Our brain is constantly working, generating more and more new associations in order to comprehend what is happening and navigate in it. Every internal and external experience generates new associations and relationships in our minds. The words on this page, grammar rules, the curses that come to your mind when my writing gets boring or monotonous; these thoughts, impulses and perceptions are made up of myriad neural connections that create the pattern of knowledge and understanding.

We HAVE TO understand. Even if we have no idea what's going on (most of the time), our brain has to create the illusion we do, not to panic, to feel safe.

The first problem here is that our perception is sometimes wrong. However, if we found some pattern before, we take it for granted and do not reconsider. Unconsciously, we don't. Although we can manually reconsider some patterns, principles and beliefs to make sure we know why we believe so.

The second problem is that it is pretty hard to change our beliefs and patterns from the outside, and it requires our constant work and attention from the inside.

Just ask yourself from time to time "why". To everything. You can define a certain day every week when you are Ms. Why, and question everything, starting from your favorite breakfast, and up to the way you treat certain people in your life. You might be mad or think negatively about somebody, but totally forget why. It is kind of funny, isn't it?

Overthinking as it is

Overthinking is basically adding extra meaning to some actions, events or situations after obsessively analyzing them over and over in your mind.

Not all overthinking is bad, and I will explain it in a moment. There is a significant difference between worrying, and being too excited about upcoming important events. Some people find it impossible to stop the constant onslaught of negative thoughts. Basically, there are 2 types of unwanted thoughts:

1. Ruminating, obsessing about the past.

For example, "I didn't have to say that yesterday to my boyfriend. He might interpret that wrong and won't see me as his wife in the future."

"Why did I refuse to go on that work trip? I could meet new people there, and have a nice experience of traveling… I make bad decisions all the time"

"Why didn't he ask me out? I was pretty sure he liked me, and then he just stood there silent. Maybe I had to offer watching a movie together or something… Ahh, Should I call him right now? or maybe I did not make it clear I am interested. Did I..?"

Such thought patterns are close to regretting and worrying about the past.

2. Making negative, sometimes catastrophic predictions about the upcoming future

"When I go to that event in this dress, everyone will see I put on weight. My boss will make a joke about it and everyone will laugh. I will be so embarrassed, that I cry and run out of the building. I will have to leave my job, be left without any income and support, and end up being poor and fat".

"If I go ice skating with my friends, something bad will definitely happen. Somebody will end up having a broken arm or leg. It will be terrible and I won't be able to ice skate again because I will be scared to have a broken arm too. I will spend the entire vacation in my room trying to push myself over there and ice skate, but in the end just feel exhausted and frustrated. I should cancel on the trip"

As you can see from the example above, worrying and obsessing about future events brings your mind to fear and anxiety. Moreover, you stress out about something that hasn't even happened yet, so basically you spoil the mood and worry about an imaginary problem. You can ruin excitement and pleasant feelings because you will expect something bad to happen, and won't be able to enjoy the present.

This is why we are learning how to stop that flow of negative thoughts and not let them spoil our evening / event / vacation / life.

First of all, you have to be able to identify these negative thoughts and realise, identify them next time it happens. Knowing the problem and facing it is the first step to recovery. You actually have to catch yourself on negative overthinking and say "STOP IT!", in your head, or aloud.

The first task is to consciously stop. The next step would be to analyse preconditions of starting that negative flow. Are you nervous? Worried about work or relationships? Are you scared? Is something important about to happen? Identify your feelings.

Do an affirmation exercise changing the negative flow to a positive one, and telling yourself how great the vacation or the work event will be.

Again, overthinking is not always harmful. Thinking too much about a certain goal or upcoming celebration is okay. The way you think about them makes a difference.

Let me provide you 2 examples of possible thoughts about the upcoming birthday party.

1) "I can't wait to have my birthday party! I am wondering who is going to come! I hope the cake will be delivered on time.. I have to call the day before and make sure they understand my time limits. Hmm.. What should I wear for the party? Not sure what dress is better -- red or green. Will show both of them to my girlfriends, and we decide on it together. It is so great I have them, they helped a lot with organization, and I appreciate they care about me!"

2) "I want my party to be perfect! I waited for it for so long, what if something falls apart..? What if people are not gonna come..? and I will stand there alone in this stupid green dress..? Or red one.. I haven't even decided on my outfit yet!! That is going to be a disaster..!!! What should i do..? Why am I so unlucky..?"

I am pretty sure you got my point. It is not okay panicking and predicting the worst possible outcomes. It is not okay feeling anxious after thoughts. It is okay to think a lot about something that is important in the moment, but try to keep it positive, try to keep it optimistic.

First, the effort should be made and a control applied, but the longer you practice conscious thinking and control over your mind, the easier it gets.

Some forms of overthinking you want to avoid:

● Second-guessing yourself

Trying to come up with several meanings (interpretations) of past conversation is one example of second-guessing. Over-analyzing, processing said over and over takes time from you and takes your energy. Second-guessing makes you unconfident and shy, searching for deeper interpretations ends up in lack of sleep and taking time from hobbies or healthy rest. Processing analysis in your head does not let you feel free from negative thoughts, and relax.

● Excessive Perfectionism (fear of failure actually)

It is okay to try to make things better, whether it is decorating the room, getting a high grade or do a decent amount of work so that the work presentation looks fantastic and easy-to-understand. It is not okay to feel unsure to demonstrate your work to somebody because of the fear it is not perfect still. It never will be.

● Fatigue

We feel fatigue when taking too much to handle for the body and mind. Burning out might be close, so it is time to slow down, pay attention to how your body feels, have a rest and let yourself relax.It is a natural way of saying - lack of energy, need a break.

● Not being able to be in the present moment

THE BENEFITS OF POSITIVE THINKING

The way a person thinks can affect the quality of her life in different ways. The development of positive thinking improves many indicators of human life. This type of thinking affects not only personal life, but also other processes and actions.

By changing your thinking to positive, there is a great chance to make your life better - achieve material success and build relationships with people around you.

Also, a big plus is a positive effect on health. With a good mood, a person perceives difficult situations much easier.

Speaking about the advantages of positive thinking, 10 points can be noted that will improve the quality of life.

1. **Health**. People who think positively simply have no time to think about various diseases. Everyone knows that self-hypnosis is a huge force that can rule. If a person does not think about the disease or, if he is already sick, is in a positive mood, then the disease quickly recedes. The psychological state has a great influence on the patient's condition.

2. **Immunity**. There has been a lot of research on the control of immunity through thinking. Subsequently, people who thought positively had a stronger immune system. Patients with negative thoughts, on the contrary, were prone to illness, and their immunity was completely weakened.

3. **Concentration**. Positive thoughts allow a person to focus on achieving goals and not be distracted by groundless troubles. It is easier for such people to work efficiently, while spending less effort.

4. **Self-control.** To achieve results as quickly as possible, it is important not to deviate from the task at hand. Positive thinking is an essential factor that helps a person to work smoothly.

5. **Making positive vibes around.** As many people say, a person is accompanied by the same emotions and circumstances she herself approaches life. With positive thinking, the right things flow into life. The facts show that positive thoughts allow you to achieve everyday goals and get quick results, while negative thoughts contribute to unfortunate circumstances.

6. **Expansion of horizons.** Thinking positively helps you see the problem from a different perspective. It might seem as not the end of the world anymore.

7. **Making people around smile.**

8. **Self-assessment.** Positive thinking allows a person to maintain a level of self-esteem. Such people respect the opinions of others, but also treat such opinions with caution. They respect their own opinions and respect themselves, their loved ones. They want to live with dignity, and they do everything possible for this.

9. **Abandonment of bad habits.** There is a misconception that positive thinking does not change life, improving its quality, but only makes a person relate to his/her life better. People with bad habits cannot make their lives better because they spend too much time on these habits. Optimists begin to think about the consequences and often rid themselves of the influence of bad habits.

10. **Reducing stress**. Stressful situations always unsettle a person. But only an attitude to such situations can radically change the situation. Anyone who thinks positively will identify useful things for themselves from the obstacles that have arisen and will work further. A negative person will spend a lot of energy and nerves on the trouble that has arisen and, as a result, will remain in the negative. Positivity increases resistance to stress in various issues.

I know changing the way you think is a complicated and comprehensive task. But look at all of these benefits. Isn't it worth it?

An art of thinking positively

No matter how confused you are, do not suddenly miss turned up offers and opportunities. Pay attention to your feelings: is there something you would like to try? Maybe some business that you've always dreamed of? Has anyone in the conversation mentioned a course, a teacher, or a book that is no longer getting out of your head? Take the first step towards what feels right and see where it takes you. And do it RIGHT NOW!

This saying is a good life slogan. Doing your best not to miss opportunities would definitely make your life journey exciting and unique, opening new hobbies, friends, and career opportunities. The movie "YES, MAN" is a great illustration. (Please, do not take a movie as an instruction, it's just an example of how being open to opportunities changes lives).

To be open to the new offers and ideas, your brain should be free from negative beliefs and statements. Why? Because when you do not believe anything good can happen to you, you mostly won't even see the opportunity, and just pass by. You were not looking for a good side of a situation, and you missed a good outcome you potentially could get. Does that make sense?

As it was already mentioned, the thoughts that come to our minds have tremendous influence on our lives. Along with and after working with adequate self-esteem, it's time to rewrite our statements and some life treatments, in order to be open to new life-changing opportunities.

Let me introduce you to a concept of Anti-Fragility, that appeared brightly in recent world literature. It was introduced by Lebanese scholar Nassim Nicholas Thaleb, currently one of the most outstanding figures in risk-management and trading. He introduced the analogy for Fragile, Non-Fragile and Antifragile events, people and activities. So, opposite to fragile (harmful or unpleasant states and conditions), the Anti-Fragility means training and effort to make life better and easier, suffering less from such damaging consequences.

For instance, when you do physical exercise, you suppose your muscles to micro-wounds, but in the long term you gain power and strength to stand more loads or look more powerful.

Approximately the same can happen to your brain and character.

And as some people are genetically likely to be of different body types, the man can be of some type of mind as well. So there are negativists, optimists, some sort of mixed type and so on and so forth.

However, as I mentioned before, no matter the initial type of mind, you can train it like a body. You know, when the baby is born, nobody knows if it can dance or sing, it all develops with time.

CHAPTER 3. In search of harmony - meditations, yoga, mindfulness

You are the most important person in your life. Try to realise it.

You are always there for you. You should have love for yourself inside, you should care about yourself, you should do pleasant things and work on your spiritual development so that You feel better.

Your interception of life is manageable. The way you feel depends on how satisfied you are with the current life. Although, this satisfaction is not always justified. See, most of the people tend to expect more, all the time. It is in human nature, we want something we cannot get right now, and worry because of one small thing, completely forgetting about all other things we already have and can be happy about.

Sometimes we take for granted things we always had, sometimes we get what we wanted and stop appreciating it the next day. That ruins harmony in life.

It is quite dangerous to always be unsatisfied with your current life, I have to admit. The reason I included this chapter to the book is that I mostly see guidelines and recommendations on how to improve yourself, get closer and then reach your purposes and dreams in self-help books, though there is one BUT. You should see a clear difference between a desire to become a better version of you, because you love yourself and want best, and constant attempts to change something because you are dissatisfied with yourself, your appearance, career and so on. That feeling can ruin you from inside. Basically, the difference is in perception and treatment to yourself here. Do you see this difference?

The motivation differs. To become a better self, or to become somebody else, because you hate yourself.

When reaching goals, pursuing dreams, it is crucial to care about your feelings, notice when you are really tired and give yourself a rest, while still having discipline. You need to pay attention to the thoughts that fill your head, and be careful if most of them are negative.

A typical situation: you live your life, thinking that you are on the right path, outwardly everything seems to be going quite successfully ... and suddenly one day you realise that you are not happy. What went wrong and when? One of the reasons might be you have never really listened to yourself and have a bad idea of your true self.

When we embody other people's ideas of success and happiness, when we do not hear our inner voice, this leads to internal conflicts. It takes persistent effort to learn to differentiate between externally imposed goals, and goals that are true for you personally. This effort will pay off. When you know how to listen to yourself, you make the right decisions personally and build the life you want. And this necessarily leads to a decrease in stress levels, increases self-esteem and brings satisfaction. Meditation is a great way to have a certain time in daily routine when you sit down and listen, learn to slow down, pay attention to your feelings and desires, and relax.

Steps that you can take on the way to understand yourself better:

1. Reflect on your values

If you do not know your true values or accept other people's values for yours, you will experience anxiety and dissatisfaction. Look back at your life and remember what has ever brought you unconditional joy and enthusiasm?

For example, if you think money is valuable, then why do you hate your job as a financial analyst, but are so happy to volunteer? Maybe it's really valuable for you not to receive, but to give?

The problem with basic beliefs is until you are aware of them, they quietly rule you.

If you find it difficult to understand whether this is your value, imagine that your whole future life will be built exclusively around it. For example, you think power is valuable to you. Imagine that from now on you will only do what to give commands. Will you be happy? Or will you feel lonely? If the second option is correct, you may value leadership, not power.

2. Realise your basic beliefs

These are your deepest ideas about the world, about other people, about yourself. It is quite possible that they were formed in childhood and inherited by you from other family members. For example, such as "The world is dangerous", "No one can be trusted", "Money is evil."

The problem with basic beliefs is that, until you become aware of them, they quietly rule you and influence all of your decisions. It is not easy to "get to the bottom" of them, it requires being extremely honest with yourself. Sometimes you need the help of a coach or counseling psychologist. But if you revisit the beliefs that drive you to wrong decisions and replace them with new ones that make your life easier, it will make an impressive difference.

3. Get to know your inner critic

Listen to the voice in your head that, like a parent, tells you what to do. His tone makes you feel helpless and humiliated. This is not your true self, it is your inner critic. He speaks in the voice of a mother or father, mentor or teacher - someone who was stern and stern with you when you were growing up. Very often he uses the words "must", "must", "need". He also likes to compare you to others.

4. Break through the chaos

One of the reasons why we cannot hear our true selves is because we are overcome by many voices. It's like tuning in to one radio station when hundreds of them are on the air. In addition to the already mentioned inner critic, we can hear, for example, our inner child ("poor me, unhappy, no one loves me, no one appreciates what I do").

How to hear yourself in this polyphony? Try this writing technique. Take a pen and throw out your worries, discontent, anger, sadness, self-criticism on paper as quickly as possible, without caring about how it is written. It's a good way to break through the chaos to your true voice.

When you know how to be in the present moment, all worries and thoughts remain outside the brackets.

At first, it will be difficult to write even one or two sentences where your real "I" will be felt, but when you practice, you can "call" it, barely touching the pen of the paper. Some people are more suited to another technique: not to write, but to say out loud everything that worries.

5. Practice daily

Another extremely effective way to get over the word mixer in your head and hear yourself is through mindfulness practice, which is best done on a daily basis. When you know how to be in the present moment, all worries and thoughts remain outside the brackets.

6. Use your imagination

If you only listen to your rational mind, you hear yourself only partially. Give free rein to your imagination – "what will happen if I ..." - and see what images and pictures your imagination draws.

7. Constantly ask yourself good questions

Good questions are those that start with "What" and "How", not "Why". The fact is that the question "Why" often leads us to self-accusations, while "What" and "How" are aimed at the future and lead to new solutions.

Don't be afraid to ask yourself crazy big questions about the future, it will help you learn amazing things about yourself. Imagine what your ideal day would be if you were a multimillionaire? If you were to spend a week with your dream partner, what would you do? If you had only a week to live, how would you use that time?

8. Try something new once a week

Many of us are confident that we know ourselves. But more often than not, we do what we were told about in childhood: this is good, it must be loved. Or what our parents did, what "all" our friends do.

The better we feel about ourselves, the better we understand ourselves.

Resist this "life of inertia" by doing something new, unusual for yourself once a week. Try some unusual exercise at the sports club or order an exotic, new meal at a restaurant. Talk to someone you would never have intention to communicate with. You will not like some of these innovations, and from time to time you will open some new facet in yourself.

9. Learn to let it go

Holding on to what you have already outgrown means closing access to your real self. This also applies to relationships. If you are surrounded by people you have nothing in common with, for a long time, and you communicate with them only because you have known each other since childhood, you interfere with your potential.

10. Take care of yourself! You, take care, of yourself

The better we feel about ourselves, the better we understand ourselves.Think about positive moments you can create for yourself this week. Maybe enjoy a fragrant bath instead of going to a boring event that is "inconvenient" to refuse? Or, finally, sit down and sort out your finances so you can stop worrying about them?

But if you are experiencing severe anxiety and therefore find it too difficult to hear yourself, consider the option of going to a psychologist or therapist. These experts know how to ask the right questions that will help you discover something about yourself that you never knew existed.

Actually, do not postpone your happiness for too long, the persvation you can refill it some time in the future is wrong. Do not postpone good things you can get today, for tomorrow.

Meditation

Meditation is a beautiful trip inside your soul, that makes you feel peaceful, relaxed, let your mind stop unwanted thoughts, and feel happy. Meditation develops spirituality, has a positive effect on mental health, strengthens self-control, and inspires for a new day.

Meditations help a lot in understanding yourself, that's like a particular time in a hectic schedule devoted to your inner, time to stop and notice what's going on with You, how you feel.

To slow down, relax and prepare for further challenges, to be in the moment.

To calm down, free up your mind.

Meditations help to find happiness inside, help to be enough, to realise what is going on and how you actually treat it.

I would also mention the **benefits** of **meditation** for nerves, and the brain.

❏ <u>Meditations reduce the level of stress</u>

Accumulated stress is one of the common reasons why a person starts meditating. Human nature has a feature of a particular reaction on danger, called "fight, or run". At that moment the body gets a sharp hormone jump, that could lead to sleep problems, depression, increasing of body pressure, getting tired quickly and a mess in mind.

Meditations help to keep the mind clear even in stressful situations and consciously choose the behavior and plan actions.

❏ <u>Meditations increase attentiveness and help to be concentrated longer</u>

The modern world presents an endless stream of information, and the human brains are often unable to proceed with all information and pay attention to everything that passes by. This is why it is important to learn how to separate the information you need from the information flow. People get so tired from constant information coming from everywhere, that they need a Break. Meditations are a great way to give your brain a rest every day, while improving concentration and having a mental silence.

❏   <u>Meditations help to control anxiousness</u>

Human brain has a section responsible for fears. It works similar to a radar that looks for sources of danger. Sometimes it gives the human a false signal (based on associations or bad memories) and causes unreasonable anxiety. That process is unconscious, and it is hard to control it mentally. But meditations can reduce the anxiety and make a calming effect on the person, when performed right.

❏   <u>Meditations help to actually realise what is going on</u>

Meditations keep you in the current moment, making you focus on your feelings and life. That increases consciousness and the effect keeps when you stand up and go to solve your problems, meet with parents, do sports and so on. Meditations bring you to the real moment every day.

❏   <u>Meditations contribute to emotional health</u>

Our brain "likes" to focus on unpleasant situations and to transfer that state to other aspects of life. Let's say you have a conflict at work. The brain works in that way that it transfers work problems to a family or relationship, and you do not realise it. People practicing meditations can better control thoughts and emotions, and do not have tha problem. While meditating, special neuron connections appear, that develop an ability to rationally estimate problems.

❏   <u>Meditations contribute to a better sleeping</u>

Since meditations unload your brain and calm down, many people observe better sleeping and feeling more energy after waking up. That way, we fall asleep faster, and the quality of sleep is higher.

❏   <u>Meditations prevent brain aging</u>

It is scientifically proved that meditations prevent brain aging by creating new neuron connections and launching brain activity. That saves you from forgetting basic things in the future, and serves as a pleasant exercise, having multiple positive influences.

You need meditations if ..

-   you do not trust. Yourself, people. If you have issues with self esteem, you are often jealous and feeling bad

-   you have this feeling that everything goes wrong, and you cannot explain why wrong, how should it go

-   you are criticizing, or are criticized often

-   you do not feel like you have a balanced and saturated life

- you have problems with concentrating your attention on one task

- you get irritated easily

- you are being manipulated

In case I persuaded you to try meditations, I recommend starting by testing different types of them and seeing which ones have the best effect.

There are three main types of meditation and many practices based on them:
• meditation to calm the mind (Skt. Shamatha), concentration of attention on breath, sounds or images;
• mindfulness meditation (Skt. Vipashyana, better known as vipassana), expansion of attention and simultaneous perception of oneself and the outside world;
• meditation of loving kindness (Skt. Maitri), directing attention on a kind attitude towards oneself, on love for living beings, etc.

There are several ways to meditate:
1. Meditation in total quietness
2. Meditation followed by calm and relaxing music, or sounds of rain, ocean waves, fire etc.
3. Meditation under guidance of the voice

You can sit, or lay down, close your eyes or open them.

To start, it is recommended to practice closed eyes meditation, since it helps to concentrate all the attention on the inside. To better understand the process and ways to relax your body and direct your thoughts, attention, I recommend starting from meditation under guidance of the voice.

You would follow the steps stated by the voice, and won't be confused on what to do next. Breathing deeply, calming down and relaxing all parts of the body will help feel safe and calm, focus attention on the feelings and associations, dreams and inspirations, help prepare for the upcoming day.

First meditations should be 5-8 minutes long, don't try sitting still for 20 minutes from the first time. The duration of meditations should be increased gradually and based on your feelings.

I provide 3 examples of meditations below, I recommend trying all of them day by day, and compare how you feel after each of them.

1. Breath meditation

This meditation leads to calmness, trains focus and concentration of attention, and helps to move away from disturbing thoughts.

DURATION
You can start this practice with 3-5 minutes,
gradually increase to 10-15 minutes.

REGULARITY
Meditate daily, 1-2 times a day.

1. Get into the correct posture.

This practice can be done both sitting and lying down. You can put a rug or blanket on the floor, or lie on the bed. Hands are as relaxed as possible.

If you are more comfortable sitting, then sit on a chair or pillow with a straight back and crossed legs.

Sit up straight, but without straining, so that your legs and body are comfortable.

2. Close your eyes and focus on your breathing.

Feel the air fill your body and leave it. Pay attention to the sensations that accompany movement air through the mouth, nose, throat and lungs.

Feel the chest and abdomen expand and fall as you breathe.

Concentrate on the places where the sensations in the body are strongest. Keep attention on every inhalation and exhalation. Just watch your breath without waiting for something special.

3. If you are distracted, gently return your attention back to the breath.

Try not to evaluate or criticize yourself. Our consciousness tends to be distracted, and the ability to notice that you are distracted, and returning attention to breathing is the basis of the practice meditation.

4. Your mind may or may not be calm.

Even if it's calm it is possible that it will be filled with thoughts or some kind of emotion. And these thoughts and emotions may also disappear soon. You may have different sensations in your body and this is also normal.

Whatever happens inside you, just watch the breath without reacting in any way, and without trying to change anything. Over and over, just return your attention to the breath.

5. Keep breathing. Keep watching.

Be in this practice for as long as you need.

6. After completing the meditation, pay attention to your condition and feelings. How are you feeling now? How comfortable are you? How helpful was this practice?

Meditation, like any new activity related to the development of the body and brain, often causes resistance. This is due to the increased energy expenditure, just like in a regular workout.

To make you want to continue meditation next time, you should not only understand its benefits with your mind, but also to experience it - this will be the main motivation for repeating sessions.

2. The practice of filling up with happiness

This practice will help you fill with positive emotions, cheer up and improve stress resistance.

It will help overcome negative tendencies of the mind, positively perceive yourself and look more optimistically at the world.

DURATION

For this practice, 4-5 minutes is enough.

REGULARITY

Do this practice 1-2 times a day.

Practice effect gradually accumulates and we become happier, stronger and kinder, both to ourselves and to those around us.

1. Get ready for practice.

Choose a quiet, comfortable place, sit comfortably (or you can lie down).

Close your eyes so that nothing outside distracts you from your practice.

2. Think back to any moment in your life when you were happy.

The moment you felt fulfilled, satisfied, and grateful. You can choose a time when you were completely protected, when you loved and were loved, when you achieved meaningful goals and received recognition - from yourself or from

other people. Or just when you were in a good place, with good people, and that's it.

3. Expand your memories.

What was the situation around, what could be observed from the place where you were?

What sounds were around you? Perhaps the voice of a loved one or the sounds of nature. Remember your sensations in the body. How relaxed were you then? What was your breath at that moment? Remember and relive the sensations on the skin. Maybe, the touch of hands or the warm rays of the sun, maybe it was a nice cool breeze.

Remember smells and collect small multiple experiences into a single, holistic experience.

4. Feel how your whole body and your mind is filled with this experience.

Feel how the happiness permeates all your cells and remains emotionally

memory. Stay in this fullness for 10-20-30 seconds.

5. Connect your memories with reality.

Slowly open your eyes and combine your experience with the feeling of where you are now. Stay some more time with this experience. Thank life

for the fact that the experience of happiness is in your consciousness and in your memory, and, keeping it in yourself, smoothly move on to your daily activities and concerns. Bring this state of happiness in everything that you are going to do during the day.

3. Energizing the brain, body and senses

This morning practice actively activates the brain and gives our body bright sensory sensations. The best time and a place for her - morning wash and bathroom.

DURATION

This practice usually takes 5-10 minutes.

REGULARITY

Do the activation practice every morning for 1-2 weeks, then optional.

The practice of activating the brain, body and senses is based on three rules:

1. You do your usual activities with your eyes closed.

2. You act very carefully, paying attention to bodily sensations.

3. You observe your inner experiences and mark them by naming them to yourself.

After you have done the practice of awakening and attunement to values - close your eyes and try not to open them while doing your everyday morning routines. Imagine the path to the bathroom and try to walk it in your mind. Then slowly get up and try to walk this path for real.

If you have any difficulties, try to feel the space with your hands, make a few small steps and get your bearings. If that doesn't work, stop, open your eyes, look around, close your eyes and move on.

1. Go to the bathroom with your eyes closed and try to do everything that you
do it normally, but with your eyes closed.

Eyes can only be opened at the end practice when you leave the bathroom.

2. Pay attention to your body and how it feels.

3. Pay attention to your emotions.

The goal of this practice is not to be able to do everything right, the goal is to activate. When our vision is disabled (and this is one of the most important sensory systems), our brain tries to make up for the lack of information through memory, hearing, touch, and so on. It triggers brain activation.

The activation of the body is associated with an increase in the activity of touch and proprioception. Some of the most strong experiences with closed eyes - sensations on the surface of the body (touch) and signals from muscles inside the body (proprioception). Many people close their eyes intuitively, when swimming, in the shower, or at breakfast, enjoying the smell and taste of food.

Try, experiment and be careful, this exercise requires being very careful!

Yoga

Yoga is a spiritual practice that often comes before meditation.

"Until you can get a firm seat you cannot practise the breathing and other exercises. Firmness of seat means that you do not feel the body at all. In the ordinary way, you will find that as soon as you sit for a few minutes all sorts of disturbances come into the body; but when you have got beyond the idea of a concrete body, you will lose all sense of the body…When you have succeeded in conquering the body and keeping it firm, your practice will remain firm, but while you are disturbed by the body, your nerves become disturbed, and you cannot concentrate the mind." — Swami Vivekananda

Today, yoga is largely misunderstood to be and is practiced primarily as asana, or physical posture. Asana practice alone is shown to have a myriad of health benefits from lowering blood pressure, relief of back pain and arthritis, and boosting of the immune system. Increasingly, many believe asana practice to reduce Attention Deficit Disorder (AD/HD) in children, and recent studies have shown it improves general behavior and grades.

And while practicing asana for improved health is perfectly acceptable, it is not the main goal or purpose of yoga.

15 reasons to practice yoga:

1. Yoga boosts metabolism.

2. Yoga improves posture. Poor posture results in multiple health issues such as tiredness, sleepiness, headaches, backaches, reduction of work energy, digestion problems. You can avoid all of them by working on posture through yoga.

3. Yoga increases blood circulation, contributes to oxygen supply to internal organs, normalizes blood pressure, reduces risk of heart diseases.

4. Yoga improves physical body condition, muscles and joints flexibility, develops resilience and control over the body.

5. Regular yoga practice cures depression and is considered a great preventive treatment.

6. Yoga makes humans happy, as it increases the level of serotonin in the blood. It improves mood and general body condition.

7. Yoga helps build a healthy body style, and as a bonus, a person can lose weight (yoga reduces cortisol and adrenaline by contributing to a calm and balanced feeling while practicing yoga, it leads to weight loss). Improvement of emotional state helps prevent overeating, and choose more healthy food.

8. Yoga contributes to a better concentration ability. Regular yoga practice improves coordination, reaction, and IQ.

9. Yoga develops fast decision making ability, improves memory.

10. Yoga helps to feel and understand the body better, improves balance and movements coordination.

11. Yoga improves sleep, calms nerves, slows us down.

12. Yoga boosts self-esteem, helps feel ourselves as a part of something meaningful, something bigger. It helps accept yourself and love.

13. Yoga is a great source of energy and power.

14. While practicing yoga, you become more friendly, kind, lovable and relieved.

15. Yoga teaches to help yourself through helping others.

Yoga philosophy lies in interconnection of body and thoughts, mood, emotions, and physical condition, what you give to the world, and what you receive from it.

While practicing yoga you most definitely notice changes in your surroundings, more open and happy people come and stay in your life, with similar interests and hobbies, life positions and views. You find new purposes and hobbies, daily routine slightly changes and now includes healthy food, time for yourself, physical exercises, meditations.

https://www.youtube.com/watch?v=sTANio_2E0Q this is a good example of yoga for beginners, you can start doing it following the voice on the video, and consider that as a first step into this spiritual practice.

I hope you made conclusions and would try practicing yoga. I strongly recommend practicing yoga in the morning, and try meditations right after yoga. That is a perfect combination.

Getting a Balanced life with the use of Life Balance Wheel

I am pretty sure most of you have met successful career people who look like robots and make an impression of a totally unhappy working force, who do not notice anything around and are just concerned about productivity and money. You should have met a kind of people who haven't found their path in earning money as well - they tried a lot of things, but still cannot answer the question of what they want. You definitely have a friend of a friend - a woman-housekeeper, who doesn't have anything in her life except cleaning, children's classes, and cooking. Or a great guy who's always complaining he cannot find the right woman.

All these examples are people who do not have a well balanced life. What I mean here is they have some aspects of their life which are fulfilled (or even overwhelmed with attention), while others - missing attention, and suffering.

Life balance is an interesting, active life according to its own rules. To be excited about life, you need to develop your skills, try new things. Every day be engaged in at least one or two activities that bring you joy. To keep life balanced, you should develop 8 aspects of life gradually and simultaneously.

You will find an example of Life Balance Wheel on the next page.

· Life Balance Wheel ·

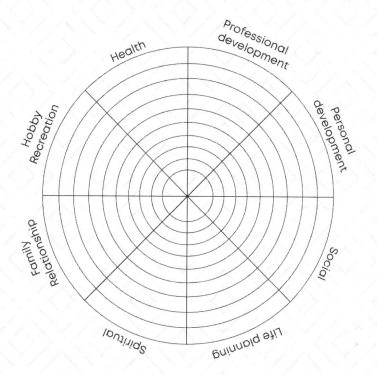

Health
Professional development
Personal development
Social
Life planning
Spiritual
Family Relationship
Hobby Recreation

As you can see, this wheel has 8 sections, equally important for life filled with sense and happiness.

You will find an explanation of each section below.

1. *Health*

Quality of food, sleep, physical exercise, body state and healthy condition of all organs, absence of illness

2. *Professional development*

The current level and speed of career development, the satisfaction from work and the desire to grow in that particular industry. Moderate loading by work, that leaves time for rest and leisure

3. *Social*
- The quality and quantity of friendship;
- The broadness of network, both professional and social;
- community interaction;
- Easiness to meet new people.

4. *Personal Development*

Developing oneself as a person: mind, skills, knowledge, habits, character, reading books, learning languages, and new things.

Cognition and development of oneself, as well as knowledge of the world, learning new things.

Personal growth - self-knowledge, culture, work on habits, the development of internal qualities, the achievement of personal perfection, the development of positive character traits;

Education - getting new skills, degrees, certificates, learning foreign languages

5. *Hobby /Recreation*

Recreation includes hobbies and passions, outdoor sports, massages, elements of self-care. Anything that involves getting rest and filling yourself with energy and resources would be considered recreation.

6. *Hobbies*
- Quality of spare time;
- Fulfillment with energy and resources;
- Family and Relationships;
- The quality of relationships with family and beloved ones, presence of support, care and love, level of commitment and involvement.

7. *Life planning*

How well the person understands what is likely to happen in 1, 2, 10 years, having plans and goals for the future.

8. *Spiritual*
- peace and harmony in life;
- the ability to discover meaning and purpose in life;
- understanding of values.

Assess the current state of each sphere from 1 to 10 points (with 1 - the lowest, 10 - the highest). 1 - inside the circle, 10 - outside the circle. As a result, you get the wheel that demonstrates how balanced your life is.

Here I want to emphasize that a happy person has a balance of these things. Continuous disregarding or failing to settle any of these aspects will eventually result in either anxiety, stress, bad mood, or feeling of waiting for life. No way I want to scare you, I just want to explain the consequences and motivate you to pay attention here, and to fill your Life Balance Wheel.

The wheel of balance gives us an understanding of satisfaction from the areas of our life. Accordingly, it demonstrates which of the sectors we need to "work" on, in order to live a more fulfilling and harmonious life, to find happiness and desirable results.

It also helps us become more aware and responsible, and take control over our lives.

In order to live a full life, you need to work on self-development, learn new things, express your personality, and your potential. It is important to establish balance and harmony in general and reach new heights in 8 aspects of your life.

Work on that persistently, and you notice how the quality of your life improves.

The "wheel of life" cannot be perfectly round - it is difficult to equally succeed in all desired areas. But it must be workable. Everyone has strengths, such as family support, bright talent or financial success. It is necessary to pay attention to sharp "failures". And the repair of your wheel should begin with those areas of life, positive changes, which will help to cope with other problems. If your health fails, depriving you of the opportunity to work fully and to rest normally, you first deal with health. Not enough money for a house, a family, or entertainment? As a matter of priority, you are looking for a way to solve financial problems.

In order to change something in key areas, you need to change your attitude towards them, your very thinking, otherwise you bury yourself in the same ceiling that did not allow you to move on before. And here you need to make an effort and force yourself to be extremely honest with yourself. Remember that everything you now think and write down for yourself - no one will see it, this is purely your analysis and your changes.

Here is my advice: have color pencils/markers with you, and fill each section of the life balance wheel with different colors, measuring your satisfaction in this sphere at this current stage of life from 0 to 10.

Dealing with limiting attitudes

We tend to ignore unpleasant facts - it's in our nature. And we do not just ignore them, but we refuse responsibility and blame the world around us for everything. It's easier to put up with what is happening. The key point is if we do not make decisions on our own to cope with problems, we will remain hostages of the situation without the slightest opportunity to change anything in our life. Let's try to understand how this happens. Let's say we analyzed our health problems and realised that their cause is overweight. Surely it disturbed us before - so why didn't we do anything? It's all because of our limiting beliefs. To find them, write down all your thoughts about such a sad phenomenon on a piece of paper: "at my age, many people are getting fat, and this is normal", "I just have such a metabolism", "I have neither the strength nor the time to go in for sports" ...

What is the picture of all these statements? The circumstances are to blame, they are completely insurmountable from this point of view, which allows you to relieve yourself of responsibility. Now that we have said this to ourselves, we have two ways. The first is the "path of least resistance" - to leave everything as it is, exacerbating problems and degrading. The second is to make an informed decision, formulate a goal, break it down into stages and act.

Getting out of your daily routine, losing your usual stability is scary. But this is the only way to change life for the better. Even if it means, for example, the need to give up a bad habit, break off a painful relationship, leave an unloved job. It is not easy, but here the vision of your goal and the search for resources comes that can give you a sufficient amount of energy.

Draw your own image

On all the paths of self-improvement, we go to the real ourselves. Try to imagine yourself having achieved all your goals, what you will become after a while. "What kind of person do I see myself as? How do I look? How do I feel? How do I express myself in life? Where do I live? Who surrounds me? What place do close people take in my life?" Of course, in some ways the fantasy will have to be tamed - it is impossible to become an opera singer without a voice. But a realistic, positive and inspiring picture will become the thing to strive for, helping you build a clear plan of goals and actions. It is important that such a picture really inspires, arouses admiration - "Wow, this is amazing! How wonderful I feel there! "

Each goal, ideally, should be specific, measurable and achievable over a certain period of time. Not "to lose a little weight", but "to lose 10 pounds by June 1, and for this I need to reduce weight by about 1 pound per week". The fulfillment of such a goal does not seem incredible, will not deprive us of confidence and strength, and will give us joy at every stage, as well as when it is fully achieved. At the same time, it must be assumed that the road is not smooth, and

64

success cannot be achieved without backtracking. There will be moments of weakness, loss of achieved intermediate results, moments of desire to give up everything and live as it turns out. This is totally normal. We fall, get up and move on. The general tendency is important. It is this satisfaction, the feeling of a positive trend of change, increased self-esteem and self-love, improved health that are important, and not at all "spherical 90-60-90 in a vacuum". Then, at every step, a new resource appears that makes it possible to move on.

The chosen goals should be exactly yours, evoke your positive internal reaction, and not be achieved for your family or some "ideal person". This is your unique life, which should not be a path of stagnation and survival, but of development: full and joyful. It's difficult, especially in the beginning, but no doubt the effort is worth it.

After it's done, look at the sections that have 0-5 scores. Write down these names of the sections in a notebook separately, and try to analyze what exactly is missing.

For example: you have "4" in the Personal Development section. That probably means you are actually doing something already for your development, like reading motivational books, or learning to play guitar; but I guess you would like to work harder on it, or you see yourself developing in 2 directions, while actually working just on 1 of them.

I had such a situation in my 20's. I was working hard on professional development, and learning foreign language, still not ranking my development as "8-10", but "5", since I wanted to draw and do swimming as well. Just didn't have time for all these activities.

So here is another question: how well your priorities are set and do you know the direction you are following.

It is easy to be dissatisfied with your life, it is harder to figure out why.

Do that. Think deep, hardly every person has an aspect where he/she is not satisfied with a current result. Find out reasons.

Then, your task is to think how, and when! you can improve the situation. Again, here we are analyzing each section separately. So if you had 0-5 in Work, Development, and Social — you are writing down your expectations and worries about each of it, and you are solving a task of how you can change it separately as well.

It's crucial for you to determine the things you can fix right away, and the problems you are not able to influence right now.

To realise your intentions of fixing the first type of things - you'll need self-control and persistence, planning and being strict to yourself (caring about the feelings still).

Now the task is not to miss problems you cannot influence right away. You NEED to decide When and How you are changing it. You need to have a Plan. For each section, for each issue.

That is a time-consuming and responsible task. I encourage you to choose an evening/day, when nobody can disturb you. Like 2-3 hours of silence and calm atmosphere. You need to focus your mind and look inside your soul. That's an amazing practice to find out both your satisfaction from your current life, And imagination of a better life, better you.

If you do it properly, you definitely will receive a couple of new purposes you haven't even thought about. That is wonderful. It means your unconsciousness will come out on the paper.

So, let's say you have analyzed aspects separately, found out reasons of imbalance and got your ways to solve it, separately.

Now the task is to combine these strategies and ideas from different life aspects into one united plan of actions. We are making a guide for you to get closer to a better life. This way, you are having a role of performer, following guidelines made by yourself.

Why is it important? A human being is not able to think about and control all aspects of life at the same time. Especially when routine tasks deadlines are coming closer, the weather is bad etc. We have to fix our treatment to life and expectations on the paper while being in the best state of mind and feelings, make a PLAN, and follow it no matter what. To do this, we need to have an exact requirement for every month, week, and day. Again, you cannot work on every single problem at the same time, but you Can choose a day and an hour for every exact issue.

The Desire map - How it works and How to make one

A desire map is a powerful instrument if made right.

Let me make it clear: Here I am not talking about any mystery, magic, and a miracle from just attaching nice looking pictures on canvas and waiting till you get it in real life.

The Desire map is about dreaming and thinking clearly at the same time and creating a visual motivator for the whole year. There are multiple approaches to making a desire map, and I will offer one of them for you, although the main thing you should realise before making one is the fact that it's not the way you make the map that ensures success, it's the thoughts and the sense you enclose to that.

How it works

First of all, it is important to have reminders about your big ambitious purposes in daily life. See, when we are dealing with everyday routine tasks we tend to forget about our dreams and purposes. And that is natural, since the human brain cannot focus on multiple things at the same time, it is much easier to deal with one thing at a time for it. When we go from one small task to the other, day after day, it is easy to forget about a dream. It might be hard to make yourself take an action towards a dream for a month or longer!

This is why you want to create so-called reminders about big purposes in your routine life to keep track of the progress and make sure you are moving forward.

Let's say you want to save some money. You'd better place stickers /fill-in boxes / any illustration of the scale to demonstrate how far or close you are to the purpose. Why? Because that might stop you from some impulsive purposes, and writing down the progress would stimulate you to keep going.

The desire map is an A3 canvas with the illustrations of your desires in several aspects of life for an exact period of time. It is scientifically proved that visual information is analysed 6 times faster than information in texts. Human beings tend to "ignore" texts more frequently than images since images are easier to perceive. Moreover, choosing an attractive image would contribute to a better mood, and at some point bring up positive associations, as well as make you get the feeling you already have an object on the picture, just for a second.

That feeling would serve as a tiny motivation for you to actually do needful to get the object.

The desire map works because it concentrates your dreams and wishes in one place. See, every day we have small desires and wishes that change throughout the day and big and small wishes are all mixed together. We make lists and visualize your wishes to prioritize, systematize them and make it easier to actually start working on them.

Make your wishes as clear and detailed as possible.

How to make the Desire map

Desire maps are unique and creative. You are free to use colour pencils and markers, paints, print bright and different size pictures, attach them in a chaotic or organized way.

It is important to devote enough time to creating a Desire map. Make sure nothing interrupts you, have about 3 hours ahead, create an appropriate atmosphere, turn on relaxing music, free up your mind.

Take a piece of paper/a notebook and start writing things you want in the coming year. You do not need to organize them for now, just make notes, try to include all the important points. Give yourself about half an hour for that.

Take a look at your list, go through it, analyze. You might want to add something or drop out of the list.

When it's done, think in terms of Life Balance Wheel sections -- where each wish or purpose belongs.

Now when you have a list of your wishes use your laptop to search for best-reflecting pictures. Print them out, and stick to the canvas. There are several approaches to placing the pictures:

- you can put your own phono in the canvas center and place pictures around
- you can place them from the most important and prioritized one to easy-getting ones
- you can form "clouds" of wishes referring to
  ❖ Development
  ❖ Health/Sports
  ❖ Recreation
  ❖ Hobbies
  ❖ Purchases

You should actually treat it as a working tool. Give your desire map some positive energy and make it inspiring in your own way. Include "real" things that can actually happen if you make an effort.

Remember that your thoughts directly influence reality, and your mood and treatment of life and its aspects play an essential role in getting your wishes to appear in real life.

Finally, put the Desire map on the wall in the room at home where you spend most of the time. That way you see it many times during the day and there is a higher chance you concentrate on it more often.

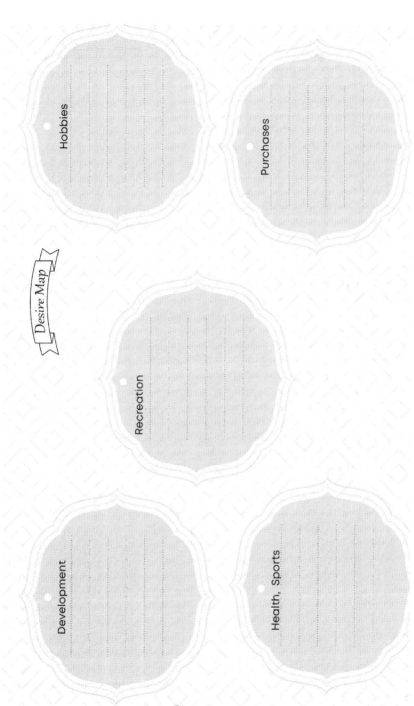

Desire Map

Hobbies

Purchases

Recreation

Development

Health, Sports

71

CHAPTER 4. Communication

Most people want to have good relationships with family, friends, coworkers etc. It is also clear that they do not happen by accident, or just because you wish them to. They are built, created, developed over time, and good skills in communication form an essential base for that amazing, close, caring and attentive relationships to happen.

Interpersonal communication is a science, and I believe an introduction to some principles and nice-to-know secrets will help a lot on the way to a general satisfaction from life and happiness, that is why this chapter is included in the book.

Effective communication means the person you are communicating with understands the message conveyed in the way in which you intended it to be understood.

The rule of 7 C of communication applies here:

❖   Correctness - the information you are delivering is clear and precise;

❖   Clarity - you are staying focused on the main points during your speech, it is easy to follow your thoughts;

❖   Concise message - you do not mention the things that could distract listener form the main idea, you try to keep your idea /story pretty short, still including descriptive elements to brighten your speech;

❖   Complete message - you make sure you finished your thought;

❖   Consideration;

❖   Concreteness;

❖   Courtesy.

Applying simple principles that are going to be mentioned here, you will be able to significantly improve communication effectiveness with your friends, in a couple, with parents and random people that come into your life. Improving communication skills might with high chance result in better academic and/or professional achievements, open new doors, and make life more exciting! Worth trying?

1. **Empathy** as an essential ingredient of a good relationship.

Empathy is the ability to put yourself in the shoes of another person, and understand what she or he is going through, how he or she feels, and attempt to look at the world from their point of view.

Empathy is a skill you can develop, the only precondition is the desire to actually be there while talking to other people, and to increase the quality of that communication. Empathy is the capacity to to have compassion and concern for others. One of the secrets of a perfect interlocutor is showing your empathy and care, but it should be natural to look convincing.

Why is it important? Every single person wants to be in the center of attention, wants to have an interesting personality to talk to, and wants to attract attention, so what we do here is we demonstrate that care and attention each person wants to get, and actually find something unique and interesting about that other person. This way, we enjoy nice conversation, and strengthen the relationship. Smartly demonstrating to the other person what we find interesting about him/her is the first thing we should do if we want to start friendship/relationship. Next sentence would serve as an explanation why we care.

2. Your **body** speaks your mind.

That is a bad thing if you are not aware of it, and a good thing if you know how to make your movements and face expressions be in line with what you are saying. This way, you will double-proof your intentions, positions, persuasions. Every smile, every frown, syllable you utter, or every arbitrary choice of words that passes between your lips can draw others toward you, or on the contrary make them want to run away.

The point is make yourself believe in what you are saying, control the way you are saying it, express your openness, or friendliness with a sincere smile, open arms and straight back, express confidence and optimism, and people will want to be around you.

3. You only have 10 seconds to **show** you are a somebody

If you are meeting new people, remember that first impression matters a lot in further communication and relationships, so make sure you make a winning impression. How? Look at the next point.

4. Charm with a smile

A secret to a magnificent smile is to

a) take a moment and look into the face of the other person;

b) pause for a second

c) try to look directly into eyes with confidence

d) let a big, responsive smile flood over your face.

This pause you make convinces the other person your treatment is personal, and that smile to his or her face is unique.

5. Eye contact is everything

Constant Eye contact is crucial to demonstrate respect and interest when listening to the other person. It is scientifically proven multiple times that a 2 minutes eye contact sends a signal of trust and deep interest to the brain, and that is an easy, still effective way to demonstrate that you care.

6. Treat people like **Big Babies**

Give the warm smile, total body turn, and undivided attention to the person you want to talk to. No pressure or anxiety should be expressed on your face or in your body gestures. You should welcome them to reach you, talk to you, want you, without no words, just a big warming smile and demonstration of being open to a contact.

7. Your **voice** is as important reflection of what you think, how much you care, and how you feel, as body language and smile. Keep your voice under control, don't speak too loud or too quiet, empathise the most important points in your speech using intonation, and speak sincerely.

Try to apply these 7 principles to your everyday communication, or when meeting new people next time, and you will be surprised how such simple rules change the way people treat you and react to your signals. Sending out "I am smiling to you, I am open to talk, to be there for you, tell me what you are like, how are you" signals by connecting your body language and thoughts to the vibes you are sending out, will result into the fact people are leaning towards you and want to get that full attention on them. This way, they are open to create a relationship and get closer.

If you want to be the person who lights up the room just by walking through the door, you better pay attention to improving your communication skills.

Communication skills and self esteem

Our ability to interact with others is built on past experiences of communications, understanding of what friendship/ relationship is, and what we represent while talking to others. Turns out, the way we behave and the way we engage other people into communication, is built on confidence and self esteem. If you are shy and timid, quiet and insecure when trying to stand out in the middle of conversation, if talking to strangers makes you feel anxious and terrified, it means somewhere in the past you have a negative experience of communication. Some people know exactly where it comes from, some do not have any clue what the issue is.

Understanding why it is hard for you to be involved in close relationships, or hard to meet new people is better on the way to fixing it, although basically you have to rewrite the scenario, change the importance and treatment to the past experience, and jump into a new one. Plus, make an effort to have at least one positive experience of meeting a stranger, making a friend, to have a base of how open and friendly you can be.

When you have a positive experience, you recall that memory and feeling, and build new communication keeping in mind positive associations appearing when thinking how great it was to meet such an interesting person and get to know him / her. Doing so helps you to stay calm and confident, smile and be open to new people, not worrying about unpleasant past experience, because now you have 2 opposite observations and outcomes, and can now choose to follow a positive pattern.

The impression you make is closely related to the way you feel about yourself, this is why it is important to find self love first, before requesting it from others. When you have healthy high self esteem, the message you are sending to the world is "Hey, I am confident, easy-going personality and I want to be friends. I am an interesting, complicated, unique person with lots of memories, hobbies, life experience and I am full of ideas. Wanna talk?".

Being able to communicate effectively involves emotional intelligence as well. Emotional intelligence consists of empathy, social skills, self-awareness, self-regulation, and motivation. Self-awareness and self regulation assure you assess your emotions, and can regulate actions to get a desirable outcome. Empathy and social skills provide a deeper connection with people you are talking to, and creates a foundation for a further involvement. Motivation is responsible for acknowledging why you need a relationship with this person, why you are having this conversation, and how much you need it.

I would say self-awareness is the most important element when it comes to interaction with other people. See, to create impression, send synchronous signals and make a united and full image of who you are to the other person, you should understand clearly who you are yourself. Moreover, when you know what your strengths are you can apply them timely and effectively.

I recommend using a visualisation instrument before an important meeting or conversation, to make yourself prepared and recall your strengths, have a certain plan and ideas you might use to make the other person interested, lean towards you . Sometimes it helps to make a preliminary research about preferences and hobbies, family and background of the other person, to have some clues how to lead the conversation so that the other person feels trust and involvement. In phycology there is a term called The effect of common knowledge. It explains that most of the time people do not want to learn new information, listen to long descriptions of something they never experienced or are far from that event, they enjoy discussing something they already know much more.

For example, if you know your interlocutor went to the same college that you did, he/she would enjoy conversation about this common experience rather than listening about your high school. Same with traveling to different countries, pets, outdoor activities, common friends and so on. When you say something familiar, it evokes exclamation "Oh, I know that!" in mind of the other person, and it makes him/her to turn their body and attention towards you.

You can try to find those points of intersection just by raising different topics and seeing the reaction, although it saves much time and increases chances of successful conversation if you know in advance what to talk about.

This rule can be applied to both professional or personal conversation, meeting parents of your boyfriend, or a new friend. Just make 10 minutes of preliminary research before meeting a person, ask common friends, search on the internet / social networks, and have a couple of ideas of what might interest the other person. Show your empathy when listening, and share your own experience in that topic.

This way, you make your interlocutor feel you two have a lot in common, and it definitely is worthy to talk again, get to know each other better!

I hope the advice provided above helps you grow a social and professional network, find new friends, and improve relationships with relatives and friends. Remember, you have to treat the other people the way you want to be treated. You have to demonstrate your interest, openness and sympathy to make the other person turn to you and smile back. Be sincere, listen attentively, and respond with optimism and confidence, and more and more people are going to want to be friends with you!

Chapter 5. Recreation

This chapter concentrates on the importance of taking a rest, rights and wrongs of recreation, how to make recreation a conscious and enjoyable process, and how it impacts working efficiently.

Taking a rest is as important as working during the day, week, or the whole year. As much as yoga represents interconnection between body, spirit and mind, work and leisure are interconnected and one does not exist without the other. Well, work exists without leisure till some point (mental burnout), and leisure might exist without work, but would not bring joy.

Let's figure out why.

Remember we talked about Life Balance?

Taking a rest is an essential part of being productive.

Human efficiency, ability to work and perform well, be creative is closely related to the way a human feels. The way the human feels is determined by lifestyle, success in other fields (sectors of the wheel), and the quality of rest.

There is nothing wrong with taking a rest. Our logic says to achieve higher results and succeed at some point, we have to work harder, more, and sacrifice other "not that important" aspects of life -- meetings with friends, physical activity, sleep. Although such an approach will eventually result in depression / bad feeling / not being able to wake up for an important meeting / mental burnout. And it turns out the time we need to recover after that is pretty much the same, as we could spend on working on the same task, but dividing time wiser. Plus, we would feel better along the way. Our body and mind need to have time for relaxation, to recreate the energy, get positive emotions, and be ready to work again.

It is important to have rest regularly, to stay tuned, avoid mental burnouts, be in the moment, renew energy and be enthusiastic about the new day.

Time for recreation is essential to slow down, reconsider ways to spend time during the day, goals, progress, have time to think and step back, look at our life and figure out, if we are satisfied.

The thing I want to talk about in this chapter concerns the ways to take a rest.

It matters and makes a huge impact on the way we feel after.

Going to a party and having some alcohol drinks, and going to the beach with friends and swimming are totally different kinds of active leisure. In both cases, you socialize, have a good time, and feel good. Although the first one undertakes going to bed late, drinking (never good for the body), and feeling a bit tired, or even worse in the morning. The second one does not have negative effects, plus makes you exercise while having a good time. Next morning you would have a high chance to be more motivated to start learning/working, then after the party night.

I am not trying to say that from now on you have to avoid going out. All I am saying is that you have to consider the specifics of each way to spend free time, and know how that would influence your productivity after.

Here is one more illustration of ways to take a rest: you can watch an interesting movie or an interview with the person that is good at something you want to be good at, or you can lay down and spend the whole evening watching TV-shows. Guess what will make you feel more motivated.

Again, you can have such TV-show nights if you like them, but you have to control the amount of them per week, and make sure you are there only when you have completed your «to do» list for the day.

Recreation makes you feel energized and ready to work productively again only when taken consciously. When you make a decision to take a rest, and choose "right" ways to do that, it brings joy and satisfaction.

All aspects of life are connected. When you do not have enough rest, feel physically bad, or disappointed with your social life - you won't be productive enough. This is why you need to hear and accept the needs your body or mind has, and satisfy them if possible. This way, you won't have a chance to become a machine that will definitely lose motivation and stop at some point, cause it will no longer feel life itself.

Recreation is important for stress reduction as well. We are living in a fast-changing, intense environment. Life is faster than ever throughout the entire history. Recreation and a calm environment is crucial for our psychics to stay healthy, and so that we feel fine.

I am giving you some ideas how to spend free time with a benefit to your mind and body:
- Any group activities like hiking, swimming, playing games, riding bikes, surfing, playing tennis
- Spending time with family
- Reading a fiction book with a beautiful view
- Taking a bubble bath, or long hot shower
- Starting the day with the things you love
- Meditating
- Having a picnic

- Being outside - having a walk in the park, listening to music or audiobook in earphones, meeting with friends
- Planning a trip
- Watching old pictures to bring up good memories
- Playing with pets
- Sleeping 8 hours a day
- Having a day without social media
- Activities that involve meeting new people
- Trying something new - food, dancing style, learning new skills, language, culture etc.
- Inviting friends over and playing table games
- Having deep conversations with people close to you
- Painting as an art therapy
- Cooking for family, friends, or yourself
- Spending the whole day doing the first thing that comes to your mind (nice experiment to reveal inner desires)
- Going shopping
- Staying the whole day in bed with a favorite book
- Yoga
- Gardening
- Decorating presents/ house/ bed

Motivation sources

Sometimes, you need extra motivation to start working and be productive, besides actual rest and physical ability to be busy again.

At this point of reading a book you probably already have a good looking and inspiring Desire map, as well as a structured and detailed list of your purposes for the year. The only tiny detail that you need to add to achieve that purposes, and make your dreams come true – is motivation. Motivation to follow the plans, work on the tasks, not just know what to do, but actually do it.

Right after you made your Desire map, created a list of purposes, it seems to you that you are motivated enough, you see clear reasons to work hard. Although, it is not that simple as it seems at first sight.

You'll need to apply both self-discipline and inspiration, motivation from inside and outside, to feel proud of results at the end of the year.

Let me give you an example here. Let's say you have a dream to write your own book. That is a long-term dream, that becomes a purpose when you set a deadline for yourself. The purpose is sophisticated and complicated, since it requires improvement of writing skills, deciding on the audience and book genre, learning about a topic you want to write a book about, and time and discipline to actually write. If you think about it, smart planning in such a situation is a must. You may spend hours and days dreaming about the day when your first book is published and it becomes famous, but that will never happen until you split a huge task into smaller parts, then divide them into weekly and daily tasks, and start working. Gradually, without excuses and laziness.

Inspiration and what I think about it

To say that short, I do not believe in seating and waiting till you feel inspired and then start working. Trust me, it does not work like that.

No denying, there are days when you simply wake up, feel much energy inside, get a couple of good thoughts, and surprisingly have some free time, and you go work on your amazing idea. But. These days. Happen. Very. Rarely.

Most of the time you would just wait for that feeling, but it would never come because what you needed to do was to start. Using self-discipline. To start because you have planned that a week before, devoted particular time and you have deadlines.

Let's say you are working on self-discipline. Having sources of motivation would make it easier for you to start every time.

I strongly recommend every person to have a list of things that

❖ inspire

❖ motivate

Why? Because when you know exactly what helps you feel better and keeps you tuned, you know what to refer to when you feel bad / exhausted / unmotivated, and that's really bad timing for that.

Here are the common motivation sources:

- A better level of life;

- New opportunities;

- Self-development;

- Providing a better level of life, or giving an important gift to family members, friends, beloved ones;

- Intrinsic motivation (treating yourself for accomplishing daily/weekly/monthly tasks). The size of treatment depends on the complicity of the task;

- The imagination about the result of your purpose (your book has been published, you are on vacation with your partner, you are driving a new car, you've been promoted and now participate in negotiations etc.);

- Taking necessary rest;

- Being around the people that motivate you. Being in the right environment is an essential part of achieving purposes. People have a tremendous influence on us, and this impact may be either positive or negative. Keep track of it, analyze, and avoid being around people that make you feel bad about yourself;

- Preparing and making a day for yourself like from the future (the breakfast you believe is perfect, great positive music, meeting friends, going on a date, looking amazing, taking a trip - whatever will make you feel good and inspire to move on);

- Hitting «rock bottom» (that is a negative type of motivation, can be a divorce, losing all money, being fired, although can be made artificially. placing yourself in the situation when you do not have a choice but growing and developing).

The most important soft skill you want to get is to know how to balance self-control, working, and treating yourself, taking a rest.

Self-esteem, self care and satisfaction from life come as a consequence.

I wish you good luck in implementing the advice from this book and making your year life-changing, amazing, and unforgettable. I hope that you will get the feeling of the desires coming true very soon!

Place to save your insights and ideas:

—

—

—

—

—

—

—

—

—

—

—

—

—

—

—

———————————————————————
— ———————————————————————
— ———————————————————————
— ———————————————————————
— ———————————————————————
— ———————————————————————
— ———————————————————————
— ———————————————————————
— ———————————————————————
— ———————————————————————
— ———————————————————————
— ———————————————————————
— ———————————————————————
— ———————————————————————
—

Place to save your insights and ideas:

—

—

—

—

—

—

—

—

—

—

—

—

—

—

—

Place to save your insights and ideas:

_____

—

_____

—

_____

—

_____

—

_____

—

_____

—

_____

—

_____

—

_____

—

_____

—

_____

—

_____

—

_____

—

Place to save your insights and ideas:

Place to save your insights and ideas:

95

―

―

―

―

―

―

―

―

―

―

―

―

―

―

―

Place to save your insights and ideas:

Place to save your insights and ideas:

Place to save your insights and ideas:

_____
—
_____
—
_____
—
_____
—
_____
—
_____
—
_____
—
_____
—
_____
—
_____
—
_____
—
_____
—
_____
—
_____
—

Place to save your insights and ideas:

103

Place to save your insights and ideas:

105

Place to save your insights and ideas:

_____

—

_____

—

_____

—

_____

—

_____

—

_____

—

_____

—

_____

—

_____

—

_____

—

_____

—

_____

—

Place to save your insights and ideas:

_____

—

Place to save your insights and ideas:

—

—

—

—

—

Disclaimer

This book contains opinions and ideas of the author and is meant to teach the reader informative and helpful knowledge while due care should be taken by the user in the application of the information provided. The instructions and strategies are possibly not right for every reader and there is no guarantee that they work for everyone. Using this book and implementing the information therein contained is explicitly your own responsibility and risk. This work with all its contents, does not guarantee correctness, completion, quality or correctness of the provided information. Misinformation or misprints cannot be completely eliminated. Human mistake is real!

Printed in Great Britain
by Amazon

74276573R00069